I0201399

Sara Makes Her Mother Proud
and Learns Good Behavior

A Parent's Guide to
Positive Proactive Parenting
for the Oppositional Behavior
of Preschoolers and
Young Children

Sherry Henig, Ph.D.

Brenner Publishing
Hicksville, New York

Brenner Publishing, LLC
P.O. Box 584
Hicksville, New York 11802-0584
516-433-0804
www.brennerpublishing.com

Project coordination, editing, graphic design and
product development by Yvonne Gray
Cover design by Lisa Pelto

First Edition Published, 2006
Second Edition Published, 2007
Printed in the United States of America

8 7 6 5 4 3

ISBN 10: 0-9777203-1-4
ISBN 13: 978-09777203-1-6
LCCN 2006905646

Preface

Positive proactive parenting involves standard concepts of behavior modification, enhanced by some ideas that I have developed over the course of my career and through my experiences as a parent. I hope these concepts will be of help to you. Please note that no techniques are guaranteed, and that the guide is offered with the understanding that the author is not engaged in the rendering of any professional services.

The ideas in this guide are illustrated with vignettes and dialogue. They do not reflect specific people or specific situations; instead, they represent a distillation of the stories and conversations I have heard over the past 25 years as a therapist and as a parent.

Acknowledgments

As this book evolved, many people reviewed it and offered me their insights. In this regard, I wish to thank my friends and colleagues who have been so kind to me in reading my many drafts and offering their valuable feedback.

I also want to extend a special thanks to the staff of the children's department of the Hicksville, New York public library for helping me solicit feedback from parents and their children; and to Joyce Oddo, for so kindly permitting me to discuss the book with the families who attended her "Jump for Joy" program.

I want to express my appreciation to my husband, Stephen Migden, Ph.D., for his constant support throughout my work on this book.

I would like to thank Lisa Pelto for her cover design.

And, finally, I would like to express my deepest gratitude to my editor and graphic artist, Yvonne Gray (www.themousetamer.com) whose enthusiasm, availability, patience, support, encouragement, and guidance made this book possible.

Dedication

To my children who have been, are, and will forever be giving me lessons in parenthood.

Contents

Introduction

Sometimes Children Misbehave

A Story About Josh

Marcia's 4-year-old son, Josh, was watching a video on TV. She asked him to put his toys away in the toy box because he had finished playing with them. Josh looked as if he hadn't heard his mother speaking to him. Marcia walked over to him and said in a sterner tone of voice, "Josh, I said put away your toys."

Again, Josh didn't budge. Irritated, Marcia stated firmly, "Josh, you cannot watch this video until you've put away your toys in the box. If you don't put them away right now, I'm going to turn off the video."

Josh stood up and walked over to the mess he had made with his toys, and started picking them up and putting them away.

A Story About Eric

Karen's 4-year-old son, Eric, was watching a video on TV. She asked him to put his toys away in the toy box because he had finished playing with them. Eric looked as if he had not heard his mother speaking to him. Karen walked over to him and said, in a sterner tone of voice, "Eric, I said put away your toys." Again, Eric did not budge. Irritated, Karen stated firmly, "Eric, you cannot watch this video until you've put away your toys in the box. If you don't put them away right now, I'm going to turn off the video."

Eric still did not budge. Karen walked over to the video and turned it off. Eric turned to her and screamed, "That's my favorite video!"

Karen replied, "You can't watch it until you've put your toys away, young man."

Eric then stood up and walked over to his toys. He proceeded to pick them up and throw them all over the den.

"For throwing your toys all over the place, you get time-out!" exclaimed Karen.

Eric didn't move. Hands on his hips and with a menacing look on his face, Eric stood his ground.

Karen grabbed his hand, marched him to his room, and shut the door.

Eric sat on his bed, seething and plotting his revenge.

Sometimes Reprimands Work and Sometimes They Don't

Most young children have their bouts of noncompliance. Losses of privileges and time-outs can often help but they do not always work. When they don't, it can be very hard for a parent to stay calm.

How This Book Can Help

The purpose of this book is to help with those times when you are trying to get your child to cooperate and your child does not want to listen.

The book begins with a little story. It is a story about a morning in the life of a 4-year-old girl, Sara, and her mother, Susan. Sara doesn't listen well, and her mother gets increasingly upset. In fact, the morning goes so poorly that it drives Susan to tears.

If you see yourself or your family in any part of the story, then read on. The book offers strategies to deal more effectively with those times when *your* young child won't listen. It will explain why penalties can sometimes provoke your child to become even more disobedient and it will explain why your child's disobedience can sometimes provoke you to become even angrier. It describes the negative cycle that can develop, in which your child's misbehavior can provoke a punitive response on your part, which can provoke your child to further misbehave, prompting you to punish, yet again, and so on and so forth cycling the two of you into further and further misery.

The book goes on to explain how to get out of a negative cycle and move into a positive cycle, in which your child will listen to you and, in so doing, will prompt you to respond in more warm and loving ways.

The formula that prompts this change often includes a positive proactive parenting strategy. This strategy is described in detail. Finally, the strategy is applied to Sara and Susan, with a very good result. Sara learns good behavior, which makes her mother proud.

A Difficult Morning with Sara

It is 5:27 a.m. at the Chernaf residence.

Susan, a young mother of two, is sleeping soundly while her husband, Roy, is brushing his teeth in the bathroom down the hall. Susan begins to feel a discomfort on her arm, which causes her to wake up. Turning over, she sees 4-year-old Sara standing at the edge of the bed poking her in the arm.

"Mommy, Mommy! Get up. Time to get up. It's morning," Sara demands.

"Oh, Sara, please let Mommy sleep a little longer. Why don't you come into bed and cuddle with me for a few minutes. It's still early sweetheart." Susan closes her eyes and immediately starts to feel the poking again.

"Mommy, I want you to get up. Daddy's up. Mommy, get up!"

"Sara, please let me sleep. Either lie down with me or go into the den and watch TV," Susan pleads.

"Get up, Mommy, get up!"

"Sara, please!"

Roy comes in from the bathroom. Sizing up the situation, he takes Sara into the den and puts a video on for her. Roy then returns to the bathroom to finish getting ready for work.

Susan can't get back to sleep, so she gets up and starts to make the bed. Minutes later, Roy comes in to kiss her goodbye.

Having straightened up her bedroom, Susan goes into the den to check on Sara. She's engrossed in the video. Susan decides to throw a load of laundry into the washing machine while Sara is busy with the video and eleven-month-old Robert is still asleep. She goes around the house, emptying the hampers into the laundry basket. Then she places the baby monitor on top of the pile and lugs the whole thing into the laundry room.

She starts a load of whites, and then begins to rub some detergent into the stained colored clothes. With the water running, it's hard to make out exactly what the sound is that's coming from the monitor. She turns off the washing machine and listens closely to the monitor. She hears little tinkly music sounds. It's the music box on Robert's crib, Susan realizes. Then she hears snatches of "Robert, Robert are you up yet?"

Susan groans to herself, "Oh, no. Sara's turned on Robert's music box. She's going to wake him up. Oh, God." It's too late, she realizes. Now Robert's up. She can hear him crying. Susan drops the stained shirt from her hands, flicks the machine back on, and runs upstairs to Robert's room.

"Mommy, Mommy, Robert is up. Pick him up, Mommy. He's up."

"Okay, Sara, Okay!" says Susan, irritated that she's in for a long morning with both kids up.

"Mom, Robert's up and I'm hungry. Make me some breakfast."

"Okay, Sara, in a few minutes. I want to change your brother. Please go down to the den and watch the rest of your video or go play in your room. I'll give you breakfast in a little while."

"Mom, I want breakfast. I want it now. I'm hungry!"

"Sara, please, please. You need to wait. Let me take care of your brother first."

Sara leaves the room. Susan lifts Robert out of his crib and places him on the changing table. "Robert, Bobert, Bobby Boo," she coos as she sets about to change him. Minutes later, Susan comes downstairs with Robert on her hip.

"Okay. Okay, Sara, what would you like for breakfast?"

"French toast."

"Okay, I'll make it right now."

Susan brings Robert into the kitchen and puts him in the exersaucer. She throws a couple extra toys on the tray to keep him busy while she warms his bottle and starts the French toast. As she turns her back, Robert bursts into tears.

"Sara, what happened?!" She sees Sara holding the plastic baby keys that she just gave to Robert.

"Sara, please give those keys back to Robert."

Sara continues to play with them.

"Now, Sara! Now!"

Sara does not respond.

"Sara, if you don't give those keys back to Robert, I'm going to take one of your dolls away."

There is no response.

Susan dashes into the den, grabs one of Sara's dolls, and comes back into the kitchen, waving it menacingly.

"See this doll? It's going to be gone in a second if you don't give those keys back to Robert!"

Sara shoves the keys into Robert's face and he lets out a cry. Meanwhile, Sara is whining.

"I'm hungry, Ma. I'm starved. I'm gonna starve."

"Just a minute, Sara!! The French toast will be ready in a minute!"

Susan tosses Sara's doll on the counter, puts the French toast on a plate, and starts to open up a jar of applesauce for Robert.

"Sit down, Sara. Breakfast is ready!"

Susan lifts Robert out of the exersaucer and settles him into his highchair. Sara plops herself into her chair and stares at the French toast. Susan notices that Sara is not eating. She's just staring at the French toast. Tears are welling up in her eyes.

"What's the matter now, Sara?"

"It's butterish… I can see it's butterish. You put butter on the French toast. You made it butterish," Sara whines.

"But Sara, it's always got a tiny bit of butter on it. I need to put butter in the pan in order to fry it. I always make it like that."

"You never do! Never!! I can't eat it! I'm gonna starve!"

"Sara, it's always like that. The butter will taste good. Here, let's put some syrup on it. The syrup will hide the taste of the butter. It will be so tasty, Sara. Here. Try it this way."

"No! No!! It's butterish! It's got butter on it!!! I can't eat it that way!!! I'm starving, I'm starving!!!"

Now Sara is crying hysterically. Robert starts to whimper.

"Okay, Sara. Okay. I'll make you something else. Just wait till I finish feeding Robert."

"I'm starving!!! I'm starving!!!" wails Sara.

"Sara, if you don't stop crying and screaming, you'll have to go to your room."

While continuing to cry, Sara walks over to Robert's walker and grabs all the toys off the tray. Robert notices from his lofty position on the highchair and starts to cry.

"Sara, that does it. Go to your room!!"

Sara doesn't move. Susan puts the jar of applesauce down, gets up, grabs Sara's hand, and drags her off to her room. She pushes Sara into her room, slams the door and goes back down to the kitchen.

When she enters the kitchen, she sees Robert softly babbling to himself on the highchair.

"Hey, Robert, Bobert, Bobby, Boo. You're a good boy. Mommy loves you."

Susan goes back to feeding Robert. She hears crying and screaming coming from upstairs, but she ignores it.

A couple minutes go by, and then Sara slinks into the kitchen. She comes over to Susan, with a tear-stained face, saying "I'm sorry, Mommy. I'm sorry."

Feeling a little more relaxed after her short break from Sara, Susan has a bit more patience.

"Okay, sweetie. I think you got upset over nothing. I'll make you some cereal as soon as I finish feeding Robert."

"Okay, Mommy."

The next hour or so goes well, and then Susan asks Sara to get dressed so that they can leave for nursery school. Sara wants to wear the stained red pants from yesterday. Susan wants her to wear something fresh from the wash. Sara cries and refuses to put on the clothes. Susan holds her ground. Finally, Sara gives in.

Once over that hurdle, they start to negotiate over the tooth-brushing ritual.

The phone rings just as it's time to leave for nursery school. Susan picks it up.

"Hello?"

Roy asks, "Hi, babe. How's it going?"

Susan bursts into tears.

Two Sides to Every Story

Here is Sara's side of the story:

"Mommy's always getting mad at me. It makes me sad. I try to be good. Robert's always good. Everybody loves Robert best."

Here is Susan's side of the story:

"I love Sara so much. But she just doesn't listen and it drives me crazy. I ask her nicely, but she won't do what she's told. She just pushes me to my breaking point. She *makes* me scream at her and punish her. Sometimes I think she *wants* me to punish her."

Types of Parental Reactions

Negative Parental Reactions

When children misbehave, parents often respond with a time-out or a loss of a privilege. But it is hard for parents not to become angry when their children misbehave, and, as a result, the consequence is often delivered angrily. Research has shown that angry punishments seem to create more resistant and oppositional children, more difficult adolescents, and more troubled adults.

Time-outs and losses of privileges have their place in the proper discipline of a child. However, they can often make a child feel very hurt and angry, especially when they are given in anger. And, when a child feels hurt and angry, she's likely to misbehave.

How Hurt Feelings Contribute to Misbehavior

It's Hard to Use Good Judgment

Let's examine how a child's hurt and angry feelings may prompt her to misbehave. First, the pain of having been punished may upset her so much that she can't think clearly. When any of us is anxious and upset, it is hard to concentrate and focus. This is so for a child, as well. When she's upset, it may be hard for her to focus on doing what her parent just told her to do, so she may inadvertently make a mistake. Unfortunately, her parents may label the mistake "misbehavior," and they may get mad at her all over again.

It's Hard to Think Clearly About the Consequences

On the other hand, the hurt child may deliberately do something to get revenge by calculatedly doing something that will hurt her parents. They hurt her, so she'll show them. She'll hurt them back. Therefore, she calculatingly misbehaves. Then her parents get mad all over again. Small children often don't think through the consequences of their behavior. In the midst of plotting out her angry revenge, the child may momentarily forget that her misbehavior will elicit her parents' wrath. As a result of her forgetfulness, she may be taken by surprise by her parents' angry response. Naturally, their anger will hurt her feelings all over again.

Hurt Children Plot Child-Sized Revenges but Angry Parents Wield Adult-Sized Punishments

A child's impulsive, childishly thought-through revenge is usually not as large as the adult-sized angry reaction that her parents are likely to have when they decide that their child has misbehaved deliberately. So her parents' angry punishment often doesn't feel to the child like it fits her crime. The child is then that much more hurt by her parents' punitive retaliation; and so she's likely to do the same thing all over again.

The Negative Cycle

A child's misbehaviors, followed up by parental punishments, can create a negative cycle. The child's misbehavior provokes a punitive response on the part of the parents; and the parents' punitive response provokes the child to misbehave. This prompts the parents to punish again, which incites the child to misbehave again, and so on and so forth, cycling further and further into mutual misery.

Punitive Responses Often Beget Negative Behavior

Penalties, like time-outs and losses of privileges, can be effective when used calmly and at the proper time. However, as can be seen by the description of the negative cycle, punitive responses to misbehavior, especially angry punitive responses, can sometimes result in an increase in negative behavior. And it's not likely that a punitive response will get parents and their child out of a negative cycle as quickly as a thoroughly positive approach.

Positive Parental Reactions

Positive Responses Often Beget Positive Behavior

Just as a negative approach may incite a child to misbehave more often, a positive response may help a child to behave properly more often. Also, a child who behaves properly will help her parents to feel warmer and more loving towards their child.

The Positive Cycle

A positive response will help to create a positive cycle, in which the child's proper behavior prompts her parents to feel pleased and proud, and the parents' pleasure and affection encourages the child to want to continue to please, and so on and so forth. In addition, just as research has shown that angry punitive parental reactions can have a deleterious impact on a child's emotional development, warm and loving parental reactions can have a positive impact on a child's growth.

From Negative to Positive

Getting out of the negative cycle in order to get into a positive cycle is obviously desirable for every family. In order to get out of the negative cycle, an event must occur that will interrupt the flow of negative interactions.

Breaking the Chain of Negativity

The chain of negativity can be broken if either of the following two events occurs:

- the parents display a moment of warmth and affection, which may inspire the child to want to comply

  or

- the child may have a moment of compliance, which may inspire her parents to be warm and affectionate

Because it is hard for parents to show warmth when their child is misbehaving, which is the first of the two options, then it may be more practical to strategize ways to prompt the child to comply, which is the second of the two options.

Compliance will occur if either the child has fewer annoying and aggravating behaviors and/or if the child has a greater number of cooperative and compliant behaviors. Both of these scenarios will probably prompt her parents to display more warm and loving responses toward her.

Decreasing the Negative

One way to decrease a child's misbehavior is to eliminate those situations in which the child is likely to misbehave. For example, if Susan arranged for Grandma to come over every morning at 5:15 a.m. to play with Sara, then Sara would probably not try to wake up Susan at 5:27 a.m. She would be too busy having fun with Grandma. This is called "distraction." If Susan permitted Sara the option to wear her stained red pants to school, then Sara would not fuss about getting dressed. This is called "giving the child choices" and "picking your battles."

Clearly, strategies that involve eliminating difficult situations are not always desirable, practical, or realistic.

Increasing the Positive

Increasing the likelihood that a child will behave properly can often be accomplished by motivating a child with a reward or an incentive. In the hopes of earning a reward, the child is motivated to behave.

Replacement Behavior

When a child misbehaves it is often the only behavior that the child could think of to use at that time. In order for a child to behave instead of misbehave, she needs to know exactly what responses are appropriate and proper. Looking at it from this perspective, a penalty may give the child a message about what behavior is *not acceptable*, but the child needs to learn a **replacement behavior** that *is acceptable*. Thus, an explanation describing what sort of behavior will earn what sort of reward provides the child with a replacement behavior to strive for in addition to an incentive to inspire the striving. Explaining what is required in order to earn the reward, as well as having an opportunity to earn it, are all part of a parenting program involving rewards.

The Promise to be Patient

A lot of parents don't like to use rewards. Many parents feel that a child should be motivated to behave properly simply because it is the proper thing to do. But of course, if children simply did what they were asked to do, then there would be no need to get them out of a negative cycle.

Furthermore, many parents would prefer not to have to resort to strategies that involve what seems to be a bribe. What's often left, then, is what most parents do all the time: they promise themselves that tomorrow they will be patient and understanding, and that they will not yell at their child. They will try to will themselves into being more patient by reminding themselves that children will be children. If something happens that causes their child to act up, they will try to summon up all their willpower to stay calm and be empathic towards their child. The idea is that a calm parental presence will help the child to regain his composure, make amends, issue apologies, clean up any mess made, and start anew with cheer and good-will, thus inaugurating a positive cycle.

If only it were so easy.

Impulsive and Irritating Behavior is Common in a Young Child

Parents are wise to remind themselves that most of their child's annoying behaviors are normal. Young children can be very impulsive, insistent, and irritating. Their drive to be independent and in control can push them to behave in ways that resemble rebelliousness. Their immaturity often results in impulsivity; their lack of life experience prompts them to exercise poor judgment. In her book, *Behavior Problems in Preschool Children: Clinical and Developmental Issues*, written in 2002, Susan B. Campbell describes how "epidemiological studies and large-scale surveys... have found that most of the behaviors... that might be considered symptomatic of disorder... (e.g., not listening, being overactive, fighting with other children, worrying, or being shy), are very common." [1]

Christopher Green, in his book entitled *Toddler Taming*, reported these results from a 1974 study he reviewed: 75 percent of three-year-olds and 92 percent of four-year-olds were described by their mothers as prone to fighting and quarreling. Seventy-six percent of three-year-olds and 75 percent of four-year-olds were described as "disobedient."

Thinking Positive Thoughts

Realizing that your child's behavior is probably normal can help you *think* more positively about your child. *Thinking* positive thoughts can help curb your anger and help you stay calm and be more patient.

However, *thinking* positive thoughts, reminding yourself that your son or daughter is still a child, and making promises to be patient, don't always work. This is because when your child misbehaves there is often an automatic, visceral reaction that compels most parents to get angry and lose their temper. It's plain hard to stay calm when a child teases her baby brother, whines about breakfast and fusses about what to wear to nursery school.

Feeling Positive Thoughts

It is easier to be more patient with your child when you really, genuinely *feel* patient, not when you tell yourself "I *should* be patient." You really will be less angry with your child when your child actually *acts* positively and *does* positive things. It's easier for you to think positive when you *feel* positive, and when your child behaves well, you will *feel* positive. When you *feel* positive, you'll act positive, and your child will likely be inspired by your positive behavior to act more positively as well, and so on and so forth. Therein lies the beginning of the positive cycle.

Motivating Your Child to Help You Feel Positive

This is where motivating your child to be compliant and to behave properly comes into play, even if it means manipulating your child, so to speak, with rewards. With the incentive of a reward, your child is inclined to put more effort into thinking through a situation in order to be able to perform the positive behaviors that will yield the reward. Then if you can see with your eyes that your child has behaved properly, you're likely to feel warm and loving. As a result, you'll just naturally be more patient.

One major goal in the use of a reward is to elicit warmth between the parent and the child. The reward serves to motivate the child to behave properly which inspires the parent to display warmth which fuels the parent-child relationship with love and goodwill which creates a rich emotional atmosphere in which the child can learn good values that lead to good character development.

The reward system is not meant to be a way of life. Instead, it's meant to serve as an occasional intervention to inspire a child to summon up the energy required to come up with an appropriate response. This also serves to get the parent and child out of a negative cycle, shifting them out of angry, hostile interactions and into warm and loving ones.

Positive Proactive Parenting Programs

A proactive parenting program is essentially any strategy in which the parent has proactively (that is, before the fact) thought through some sort of plan in which to give some sort of reward or some sort of penalty. A *positive* proactive parenting program is a strategy that involves a reward for appropriate behavior instead of a penalty for inappropriate behavior.

The Reward

The Reward Doesn't Have to be a Big Deal

Incentives and rewards can be as small as check marks and as large as new Barbie dolls. Everything in the middle counts as well, including smiley faces, sticker charts, staying up an extra half hour and playing catch with Dad.

Type of Reward

The type of reward you use will have a major impact on how successful you are likely to be with your positive proactive parenting program. Since every child and every family is unique, each reward has a different value for each child. Some children are motivated by a parent's warm pat on the back. Other children couldn't care less. If the reward you choose for your positive proactive parenting program doesn't work out well, you may want to pick a different and perhaps more special reward.

Frequency of the Reward

The frequency with which a reward is given also figures importantly into whether your positive proactive parenting strategy will work. You can give a reward once a week, once a day, several times a day, or several times an hour. When your proactive parenting strategy doesn't work the first few times, you may want to pick a different frequency with which to give the reward.

Regaining the Use of a Reward

Sometimes parents are resistant to using rewards because they feel that their child already has enough toys and treats available. Sometimes parents will notice that no reward seems to be special enough to inspire their child to comply. Thus, there are occasions when it may be worthwhile to take away some of a child's standard treats (like full-time use of a TV or video game system, or the use of the dolls and doll clothes.) Then the parents can have "regaining the use of these treats" as the reward.

This procedure needs to be done delicately so that it doesn't come across like a penalty. One way you can do this is to have a quiet discussion with your child at the end of the day; something like the following:

"You know, sweetheart, it's been so difficult for you to leave your brother alone when he bothers you. So I've been thinking, how about if we see if you can make it until breakfast without hitting him. If you can, then you can play with your dolls. I'm going to put your dolls away tonight so that you can earn them back tomorrow. Show me that you can keep from hitting your brother and then we'll get the dolls out so you can play with them."

If your daughter starts to fuss, which she very well might, then you can put a positive, but firm, spin on the idea.

"Honey, you can definitely play with your dolls. However, I need to see that you can play nicely with your brother without hitting him first. Show me that you can avoid hitting him tomorrow morning, and then you can play with your dolls."

If she continues to complain, then change the subject, walk out of the room, do the dishes, or do anything else you usually do to try to avoid letting a difference of opinion escalate into a fight.

Advance Preparation

Thinking up the Reward in Advance

You are not likely to think of a good reward or a proper frequency with which to dole out the reward on the spur of the moment. Since you need to be absolutely certain that whatever reward you offer is something that you can and will deliver in an absolutely timely manner, you'll need to be proactive and think it through in advance.

Preparing You and Your Child for the Reward Program in Advance

Positive proactive parenting programs work best when you thoroughly discuss the program with your child in advance. Your discussion should be upbeat so that your child is excited and eager to participate in the plan. Moreover, when your child misbehaves, thereby not earning the reward, you need to remain calm. You'll ruin the whole thing by blowing up. If she doesn't get the reward, you'll need to put a positive spin on the situation and remind her that she'll have lots more chances later in the day to earn a reward. This will be hard to do because your child has misbehaved, which probably has you angry and stressed out. You need to prepare yourself, in advance, for how you're going to deal with your child's misbehavior in a warm and understanding manner despite your anger, so that you can actually pull off being warm and understanding when you're ready to explode.

Two Different Mornings

A Morning Without Advance Preparation

Sara's been up for a half hour. She's annoyed that Mommy wouldn't get up for her right away. She's upset that Mommy wouldn't start breakfast right away. And she's angry that Mommy seems to be paying so much attention to Robert. She's hungry and cranky and all wound up. She's in a tizzy. She's nearly irrational. And Susan's patience is worn out as well.

"Mom, I'm hungry, I'm starving! I want you to make the French toast *right now*."

Susan reminds herself that Sara is only four. She lectures herself to be patient.

"Sara, you have to wait. It takes time to cook."

"I'm hungry, I'm starving! I'm starved!!!"

Susan decides to entice Sara to calm down with an incentive.

Do you think Sara will calm down if Susan offers her a reward at this point, after she's gotten herself so upset?

"Sara, just be patient. I'll give you a sticker if you calm down."

Sticker, schmicker! Once Sara's gotten herself this wound up her tantrum probably won't let up. When children are this worked up they often can't think rationally. Even offering a trip to Disney probably will not change the mood. They just want what they want and they want it now.

"Mooommm, I want my French toast now!!!"

If Sara doesn't quit whining, and if Susan hasn't thoroughly prepared her own positive spin, then Susan's likely to respond like this:

"That's it! No sticker for you. Just be quiet already! I can't stand your screaming!"

A Morning with Advance Preparation

Susan and Roy decided to try a sticker chart to encourage Sara to behave properly in the morning. They spent a half hour last night discussing this positive proactive parenting strategy. They decided that Sara could earn up to four stickers a day; one for each of the following behaviors: no waking up Robert when Robert is sleeping, no whining for breakfast, no fussing over what clothes to wear, and no hitting or shoving Robert.

They discussed it with Sara before bedtime over cookies and milk. They asked for her input and made sure she was excited about the idea.

First thing in the morning, Susan reminded Sara about the sticker chart and, every several minutes or so, she let Sara know that she was on her way towards earning a lot of stickers and a nice prize at the end of the week. Sara was psyched.

Then, when Sara started to whine about breakfast, Susan turned to her and said, "Sara, remember, you can put a sticker on the chart on the fridge after breakfast if you can just be patient and not whine. Why don't you go take a look at the chart and figure out where you'd put the sticker."

Sara had not gotten herself worked up yet, so this had a good chance of motivating Sara to be quiet. Certainly, a much better chance than in the previous example.

Proactive is Better than Reactive

In other words, there's a better chance that your child will behave properly if you handle the reward program proactively, meaning you are prepared and you have discussed it in great detail in advance.

If Sara hadn't stopped whining, Susan's preparation would have helped her to remain calm and stay upbeat. She would have anticipated Sara's bad reaction, and she would have prepared herself to be calm.

"Okay, Sara. You didn't stop whining so you don't get the sticker. But don't worry, honey, you still have a chance to earn stickers for not waking up Robert, for getting dressed without a tantrum, and for not hitting your brother."

Positive Proactive Parenting Plans for Sara and Susan

Ten Examples

1. Susan can make up a checklist. The daily checklist might look like this, with pictures along the top to illustrate the desired behaviors:

	Waited quietly for breakfast	Got dressed with no fuss	Played with Robert without hitting him	Took night-time bath with no fuss
Mon.				
Tues.				
Wed.				
Thurs.				
Fri.				
Sat.				
Sun.				

At the end of each day, Sara can count up her checks and exchange them for rewards. She can do the same at the end of the week. If that doesn't work well, Susan can consider different rewards.

If that still doesn't work well, she can consider a different frequency in which Sara can earn checks and receive rewards. For example, Susan can make

31

up three separate checklists; one for the morning, one for the afternoon and one for the evening. If that doesn't work well, she can try an even more frequent frequency, such as three checklists for the morning alone.

The following are samples of a daily reward menu and a weekly reward menu:

Sample Daily Reward Menu	
Three checks in one day:	Sara gets to watch a special video Or Sara gets one game of cards with Mommy.
Four checks in one day:	Sara gets both of the above.

Sample Weekly Reward Menu	
20 checks in one week:	Sara gets to have her fingernails painted Or Sara gets to buy some special clips for her hair.
25 checks in one week:	Sara gets to do both of the items above Or Sara gets to go out for a movie and an ice cream with Mommy or Daddy.

2. Susan can make up sticker charts just like the checklists. Instead of putting boring checks on the charts, to be exchanged later for rewards, Susan can put all sorts of cute little stickers on the charts. If Sara doesn't respond to just having charts with cute stickers, then Susan can have sticker charts in which there is an opportunity for Sara to exchange a certain number of stickers for certain types of rewards. If that doesn't work, then Susan can try varying the frequency with which she gives out the stickers, just as she did with the checkmark check-lists.

3. Susan can buy a cute stamp from a stamp store, stationery store or toy store. She can tell Sara that she'll get her hand stamped every time she accomplishes one of the behaviors that Susan will post on a list on the refrigerator. Susan can stamp the list on the refrigerator in addition to stamping Sara's hand.

4. Instead of the stamp idea, Susan can buy adorable little washable tattoos and tattoo Sara instead of stamping her.

5. Susan can buy some tiny gold stars to stick on a chart, on the back of Sara's hand, or on Sara's clothing. She can reward Sara with a gold star every time Sara performs one of the proper behaviors listed on the refrigerator.

6. Susan can buy some pebbles from a home improvement store or a garden store (or she can get them from her backyard.) She can then take a jar

and use a magic marker to mark the jar with lines. Each time Sara does something from the list on the fridge, she can put a pebble into the jar. When there are enough pebbles to reach a line, then Sara gets a chance to do one of the following:

1. Polish her nails.

2. Go to a toy store and pick out a little reward.

3. Pick out a little reward from a shoebox filled with assorted items from a 99-cent store.

7. Susan can carry poker chips around in her pocket. Each time Sara does something from the list, Susan can take a chip out of her pocket and put it in a jar. Sara can collect the chips at the end of the day and exchange them for something in a goody bag that Susan and Roy have proactively put together.

8. Susan can make up a list of activities such as the following:

1. Play one game of "Go Fish" with Mommy.

2. Play tag in the backyard with Daddy for 10 minutes.

3. Have a tea party with Mommy.

4. Stay up an extra half hour at night.

5. Look at Mommy and Daddy's wedding album.

Then Susan can write each activity on a 3 x 5 card. Each time Sara does something from the list, she will be allowed to pick one card from the pile of cards and be given the opportunity to have the treat described on the card.

9. Susan can identify just one behavior from the list and she can put all her effort into encouraging Sara to learn just that one proper behavior. For example, she can choose "playing nicely with Robert without hitting him." If Sara is well-behaved all day (by not hitting Robert, in this case,) then she could be allowed to look at her baby pictures at night, she could get a bedtime snack, or she could get two bedtime stories instead of one.

10. Susan can tell Sara that if a certain portion of the day goes well, then she will get a special treat at the end of it. For example, she can tell Sara that if the morning goes well, then she can choose to do something special for lunch, like go to a fast food restaurant or a restaurant with a little indoor amusement section in it. Susan can tell Sara that "going well" means letting Robert sleep, playing nicely with him without hitting him, not whining about breakfast, and brushing her teeth when asked.

Principles of Successful Positive Proactive Parenting Plans

I could come up with 10 more ideas, and so could you. Just remember the following principles of successful positive proactive parenting plans:

1. You need to be absolutely sure that you can follow through, in a most timely fashion, with the reward that you choose.

2. You need to prepare your child in advance by discussing the plan with her and by giving her plenty of reminders about her reward program. This way, she'll be primed to behave properly, and, if she doesn't behave properly, she'll at least be better prepared for not receiving her reward.

3. You need to stay calm and upbeat if your child misbehaves. This helps your child to experience you as benign and benevolent despite the fact that you did not dispense a reward.

Once again, you must make absolutely sure that you can follow through with any incentive that you discuss with your child. You'll be taking two steps backward rather than one step forward if your child gets all excited about a reward, earns it, and then doesn't get it. You will simply be showing her that you are unreliable or untrustworthy. She won't believe in you and she won't be as inspired to work for the reward the next time. Your campaign is to improve your relationship with your child and instill love, admiration and a desire to please you. Lack of trust will destroy your campaign and spoil your relationship with your child.

A Good Morning with Sara

The Chernaf Family Tries
a Positive Proactive Parenting Plan

Here's how the morning might unfold when the Chernaf family uses a star chart that they will review at the end of the day.

Susan's been proactive. She's talked about the chart with Sara and Roy. Everyone's prepared for the fact that Sara may wake up early. Roy knows to listen carefully for sounds that Sara might be awake. If she gets up, he'll take her to the den and put on a video for her. If she's hungry, he'll give her a bowl of cereal.

It is 5:27 a.m. at the Chernaf residence

Sara wakes up. She gets out of bed. She walks by the bathroom. Dad sees her. He calls out to her, "Good girl. You're remembering not to wake up Robert. Come in and keep me company. Let me finish shaving and then I'll put in a video for you." She watches with interest while he finishes up, and then they both trot down to the den so he can put in a video. At 6:20, Roy kisses Susan goodbye and goes off to work.

Susan gets out of bed and goes down the hall. Sara is not in her room and Robert is sleeping. She goes into the den and sees Sara watching a video.

"Sara, I'm so proud of you. You let me get my sleep. You're such a good girl!" Sara beams.

"Sara, could you please either stay down here or play quietly in your room while I put in a loud of wash? I'd like to get the laundry started before Robert wakes up. Remember, you get a star if you can keep from waking up Robert."

"Okay, Mommy." Sara looks confident and proud of herself.

Susan whips around the house collecting the laundry from the hampers. Then, with a full laundry basket, topped with the baby monitor, she enters the laundry room and starts the wash. Minutes later, she emerges, with the monitor in her hand. She goes over to the den.

"Sara, you're still watching the video? I'm so proud! You didn't pester me and you didn't wake up Robert. You've already earned a star this morning. Wow, you're doing great."

Sara beams.

Suddenly, they both hear Robert cooing from the monitor. They go up the steps to his room and peek in. He is up. Sara goes over to the crib and peers in. "Robert, Bobert, Bobby Boo." He gurgles. She gently tickles Robert with one of his stuffed animals. He laughs and smiles at her adoringly. She smiles back.

Susan gets a warm, fuzzy feeling and thinks, "It's great being with my two little babies."

Epilogue

Proactive Parenting Programs Really Can Work This Well

Does this sound too good to be true? Well, you'd be surprised. If Susan and Roy are very proactive and work very hard to stay calm and upbeat, and if Sara's temperament is not compromised by a psychiatric disorder, then there is a fairly good chance that the positive proactive parenting plan will come out this well. By the way, these techniques can help with children who have serious emotional and behavioral problems as well, though the child may not respond quite as quickly or quite as well if the child's problems are rather severe.

Of course, it's certainly possible that the morning might not have gone this well the first time. If it hadn't, Susan and Roy could come up with something a little more exciting than a star chart, or they could dole out the stars more frequently, like every few minutes or so.

There are lots of different ways to motivate children with incentives and rewards. There is definitely a time and place for penalties but, when a negative cycle gets going, it often helps to try out a positive proactive parenting program to gets things back on a positive track.

You Won't Have to Use Positive Proactive Parenting Programs Forever

Don't worry that you'll have to spend the rest of your life using rewards to get your children to do the right thing. That doesn't have to happen. These reward programs tend to fade away, and the child's natural aging process brings about new and different challenges that require different approaches. For many behaviors, once the child gets the hang of it, it will become second nature to do it. How many people continue to need rewards for the rest of their lives in order to use a toilet?

Anyway, it's not really just the reward that causes the good behavior to persist. The sweet, warm feeling inside the family's heart that keeps the whole positive cycle going, significantly contributes to the child being inspired to do the right thing.

When things get back on track with your child, you'll notice that you'll have more patience. Your child will sense your patience and will be more inspired to please you. The more he pleases you, the more patient and loving you'll be. Then you've got that positive cycle going.

Your positive cycle may not be very intense and it surely won't last forever. Nevertheless, every little short-lived positive cycle helps ward off a negative relationship with your child. Every time a positive cycle starts to deteriorate, you can always try to bring it back with a new and different kind of positive proactive parenting program.

I hope these ideas are helpful to you when you and your child get into a negative cycle. On the next page is a reading list of wonderful books for parents of young children. Good luck.

About the Author

Sherry Henig, Ph.D. is a psychologist with a private practice in Jericho, New York, who has written books for adults and children. She lives on Long Island with her husband and children. Learn more about her at www.sherryhenig.com.

Suggested Readings

Brazelton, T. Berry. *Toddlers and Parents*. New York, New York: A Delta Book. 1974.

Fleming, Don with Balahoutis, Linda. *How To Stop The Battle With Your Child*. New York: Prentice Hall Press. 1987.

Garber, Stephen W.; Garber, Marianne Daniels; and Spizman, Robyn. *Good Behavior*. New York: Villard Books. 1987.

Goldstein, Sam; Brooks, Robert; and Weiss, Sharon. *Angry Children, Worried Parents*. Plantation, Florida: Specialty Press, Inc. 2004.

Green, Christopher. *Toddler Taming*. New York: Fawcett Columbine. 1984.

Harris, Clemes and Bean, Reynold. *How to Discipline Children Without Feeling Guilty*. Los Angeles, CA: Price, Stern, Sloan. 1990.

McKay, Matthew; Fanning, Patrick; Paley, Kim; and Landis, Dana. *When Anger Hurts Your Kids. A Parent's Guide*. Oakland, California: New Harbinger Publications, Inc. 1996.

Pearson, Linda. *The Discipline Miracle*. New York: American Management Association. 2006.

Peters, Ruth. *It's Never Too Soon.* New York: Golden Books. 1998.

Schaefer, Charles and DiGeronimo, Theresa. *Teach Your Child to Behave. Disciplining with Love, from Two to Eight Years.* New York: Penguin Books. 1990.

Severe, Sal. *How to Behave so Your Preschooler Will, Too!* New York: Penguin Putnam, Inc. 2002.

Shiller, Virginia with Schneider, Meg. *Rewards for Kids! Ready-to-Use Charts & Activities for Positive Parenting.* Washington, D.C.: The American Psychological Association. 2003

Turecki, Stanley. *The Difficult Child*. New York: Bantam Books. 1985.

Wolfe, Jerri. *I'm Three Years Old*. New York: Pocket Books. 1998.

Wyckoff, Jerry; and Unell, Barbara. *Discipline Without Shouting or Spanking. Practical Solutions to the Most Common Preschool Behavior Problems*. Deephaven, Minnesota: Meadowbrook Press. 1984.

Notes

[1] Campbell, Susan. *Behavior Problems in Preschool Children.* New York: The Guilford Press. 2002.